Fifteen

original story by
Jennifer Degenhardt

Translated by
Sydney Bartholomew

Edited by
Hannah Pitkofsky

Cover art by
Morgan Jensen

This story is a work of fiction. While the characters are products of the author's imagination, some places mentioned in the story are real.

To all of those getting to know children or
parents for the first time.

CONTENTS

ACKNOWLEDGMENTS

At the time of publication (or at the time of art creation), all of the collaborators on this project were students in high school, either commissioned or through an internship. It is an honor and a pleasure to provide an opportunity for young people to gain some experience by using their skills and talents.

Thank you to Sydney Bartholomew for the translation from Spanish to English. The bilingual program served you well!

Thanks also to Hannah Pitofsky for reading through the manuscript and making it read naturally in English.

Special thanks to Morgan Jensen for the amazing artwork for the book's cover. Artists of all ages amaze me, but student artists most of all.

Chapter 1
Ximena

It's eight o'clock at night and I'm alone in my room. My younger brothers, Javier and Joaquín, are asleep in their room and my parents are in the kitchen.

As usual, I'm writing in my diary. It's a new diary. The pages are many colors: red, yellow, orange, blue, and green. I write in it every night about the events of the day, and personal things too.

Tonight I'm writing at my new desk. The desk is small and white, but it's really pretty. My dad made it and gave it to me for Christmas a week ago. He is very talented. He makes a lot of furniture in his workshop.

I am just about to write on the first page of my diary when I overhear a conversation between my parents:

"But Marisol, he IS her father," my dad says.

"I know, Federico, but I don't know if she should be in contact with him," my mom says.

"Marisol, the letter says that he's in a lot of programs. He's different now," my dad says.

"But he wasn't good before. Not for me, not for..."

"Marisol, Ximena needs to be in contact with him," my dad says. "It's really important."

What?! My parents are talking about my FATHER. My biological father.

Federico isn't my biological father but he is the only one I've ever known. My mom and Federico got married when I was four years old. I was the maid of honor for my mom. I wore a very pretty pink dress with lots of flowers on it. Princess...on that day my dad called me princess, and he still calls me his princess now.

My mom never talks to me about my biological father. Ever. And now there's a letter? What could it say? I want to know.

I have a lot of questions, but I don't want to say anything right now, so I write in my diary instead.

Dear diary,

Today was an interesting day...

Chapter 2
Daniel

It's nine at night and I am in my "room" with another guy. His name is Johnny and he's new here. Johnny is on his bed. He doesn't say much because he's listening to music with his headphones. Johnny is my brother, but not my biological brother. He is my brother of circumstance.

The noise is awful here, but that's normal. It's really loud — so loud that I can't concentrate.

I'm at my desk. In our room there is only one desk. It's made of metal, and it's part of the wall. The beds are metal too, and they are one on top of the other, bunk beds. There is only one small window and it has bars on it. The door is heavy and it's locked with a key.

Johnny and I are here with 3,500 of our "brothers." We all live in rooms that are really cells. We are prisoners of Dudley

Correctional Center, which is about 50 miles from my hometown of Encinitas.

Yes, I am a prisoner, but I am a father as well. I have a daughter. I can't believe it. I have a daughter who is 13 years old. Incredible. My daughter Ximena...

"Daniel!" yells another brother who is at the door with the mail, "I have two letters for you."

"Thank you, Bear." I say as I take the letters.

Bear is not his real name. I don't know what his real name is, but here in Dudley we call him Bear.

I return to the desk. I don't have much contact with my family, but my aunt always sends me letters and photos of Ximena. Ximena lives with her mom and her mom's husband.

It's been two weeks since I've written to Ximena's mom asking permission to write to my daughter. But the letters that Bear gave me aren't from Ximena's mom. I am going to have to wait longer for a response.

The letters are from the State of California and they contain legal information. They are important, but I don't want to read them right now, so I decide to write in my diary.

Dear diary,

For eight months I have been working in many different programs. In the future, I want to show my daughter that I am a different person than before. As a teenager I was...

"Lights out," the guard says.

There isn't any more time to write. There is only more time to think. But it's hard to concentrate because the noise is so awful.

Chapter 3
Ximena

I'm thinking about the conversation my parents had about my biological father the other night...

"Ximena," my mom yells. "Let's go. We only have two hours to go shopping."
"I'm coming, Mom."

My mom and I are going shopping today. My cousin Paloma's *quinceañera* is in two weeks, and I need a new dress. I have an idea of what dress I want. It's long and blue and...

"Ximena," my mom says. "Pay attention. First we'll go to Flashbacks and then to the Community Resource Center."
"Mom, I don't want to go to Flashbacks or the Community Resource Center. I want a new dress."
"I understand, Ximena, but you know our family doesn't have much money. And with so many *quinceañeras* that you need to go to..."

"Yes, Mom. I understand. But, I don't even want to go to Paloma's *quince*."

"Me neither. But we have to," my mom says.

Paloma is my uncle Jorge's daughter. He is my mom's brother. My aunt Rosario, Paloma's mom, is...well, she is too much. She wants everything to be perfect. I don't like her. And I don't like Paloma much either because she's exactly like her mom.

First we go to Flashbacks. The woman that works there is my mom's friend. Normally she has a good selection of dresses, but because it's spring and prom season, she doesn't much. And the dresses that she does have, I don't like.

"Okay, Ximena. We'll go to the Community Resource Center," my mom says.

I am not happy. I want to find a long blue dress. I want a princess dress...

My mom and I spend half an hour in the next store. There is a blue dress there, but it's not the dress of my dreams. It's fine. I don't want to cause any problems with my mom. She is stressed today.

"Do you want ice cream?" my mom asks.
"Yes, but..." I say.
"I need to talk to you. Let's share a sundae at Handle's?" my mom says.

I wonder what she needs to talk to me about...

Chapter 4
Daniel

I arrive from my job in the prison. I work in the laundromat. Along with ten other men, we wash the clothes for all of the people in Dudley. The work is boring, but they do pay me 40 cents per hour.

I only have fifteen minutes to get ready. I have to go to my technician class for heating, ventilation and air conditioning (HVAC) installation and repair during the afternoon today. In a month I'll be finished with the program and I'll earn a degree. I can't wait to get a new job here in Dudley, hopefully one that pays better.

Johnny is in the cell. He's listening to music as usual. But today he has a question, "Daniel, do you like to study? Why are you taking those air conditioning classes?"

"Dude, I only have a year and half more here. When I leave here, I want a job. I want to be a part of my daughter's life. I still don't know her."

Right then, Bear arrives at the door with a letter for me.

"Is this the letter that you're looking for, Daniel?" Bear yells. He yells because there is so much noise.

I look at the envelope. The return address is where Marisol lives with her husband, Ximena and two other kids.

I take the letter and I sit on my bed. I am both excited and nervous. I open the envelope and I start to read.

Dear Daniel,

Thank you for not being angry with me. You should get to know your daughter and she wants to know about you. Ximena is a sensible girl and very smart. She is growing up. Being in touch with her is going to help her. And Daniel, thank you for writing to me first. It's clear that you have changed.

Mari

I put the card in the envelope and run to my class. I am very, VERY happy.

Chapter 5
Ximena

My mom and I are at an ice cream shop, Handle's, and she explains everything about my biological father.

"Ximena, your biological father is in Dudley Correctional Center," my mom says to me.

"Why? Where? What happened?" I ask her.

"Thirteen years ago, your father and his friends were in an accident. A woman in the other car died. Your father was the one who was driving that night and he had to go to prison for fifteen years."

"But it was an accident, right?" I ask. "Seems like that's a lot of time in prison for an accident."

"The circumstances were serious. I will explain it to you another day. But I want to tell you that your biological father, Daniel, wants to contact with you. He wants to write you a letter. Is that okay with you?" my mom asks me.

I don't know what to say. Finally, I know where my dad is and why, but...do I want to have a relationship with him?

"I'll think about it, Mom."
"Okay, Ximena. It's your decision," my mom says.

I almost forget about the blue dress and the ice cream. My reality is going to change a lot. What am I going to do??

I have a big decision to make...

Chapter 6
Daniel

One morning before going to work in the laundry room, one of the prison guards stands in the door.

"Daniel, the warden wants to talk to you."
"Oh, ok. Do you know why?" I ask.
"No. But you need to go now."

I take my jacket and I go with the guard to the warden's office.

In the office there are nine other inmates. Inmates, yes, but good men. Like me, they are enrolled in a lot of programs and they want to change.

"Good morning," the warden says. "You all are here because I want to offer you a chance to participate in a new program at Dudley. We're going to work with an animal shelter training dogs, specifically the ones that have been in the shelter a long time."

No one says anything. Is the warden serious? Will we really get to work with dogs?

The warden continues, "This program is special because you all will get to live with the animals 24/7. The dogs need to learn so much. You all are the best candidates for the program. BUT," the director yells, "if there is any problem with any of you, you will not be able to participate any longer. Is that clear?"

The warden then asks if everyone wants to participate.

We all say yes.

*****

It's nighttime and I am very tired after working and going to my classes. In a month I will be even more tired because I will have a dog with me all time. I need to study for my HVAC test. But tonight, I have something more important to do: write a letter to my daughter.

Dear Ximena,

I would like to introduce myself. I am Daniel...

Chapter 7
Ximena

It's the day of Paloma's *quinceañera*. Everyone in my house is getting ready. My mom puts on an old, pink dress, and my dad and my brothers are wearing blue pants, white shirts, and ties. The boys don't like the ties.

"Mommy, I don't want to wear a tie," Joaquín says.
"Me neither," Javier says.
"Boys, please. It's only for a few hours," my mom says.
"Come here, boys. You guys are so handsome. You will be the most handsome at the party," my dad says, patting the shoulders of each of my brothers.

My dad is a calm man, and his words always calm my restless brothers.

I look one more time in the mirror. I want to smile, but I don't like the reflection. My dress is ugly. At thirteen years old (almost fourteen), my hair is awful and I look awful.

I want to cry. I don't want to go, but I can't say anything. I hear my mom saying, "Paloma is your cousin and it's important to celebrate with her" — a phrase that she's said to me so many times recently.

Ugh. Perfect Paloma. I want to throw up.

*****

First, we arrive at church. The whole family on my mom's side is Catholic and celebrates the *quinceañeras* with a special mass. Normally I enjoy going to mass at church, but today I don't want to because I don't want to celebrate Paloma's *quince*. When we arrive at the church, from the car window I can see her with her parents and godparents. They go up the stairs to get to the front door of St. John's Church. Paloma is wearing a pink dress. Her hair and her makeup are perfect. She looks like a princess. She's beautiful.

Behind Paloma, her parents and her godparents follow the girls and boys Paloma has chosen for her *quince* court. These boys and girls are her court of honor and are Paloma's friends. The girls are all talking, and some are having problems walking with their high heels and big dresses. The boys aren't talking much, and they look uncomfortable in their formal clothes.

"Let's go, Ximena," my mom says. The mass is going to start."

We get out of the car. My dad notices that I'm not very happy and stops to talk to me.

"Ximena, you look beautiful today. I love the color of your eyes. Let's go. Are you going to dance with me at the party?"

I smile and respond, "Dad, yes I will dance with you, but, please, you can't dance like a crazy person, okay?"

My dad works a lot and a lot of the time he is really serious. But he likes to dance to all kinds of Mexican music: *Sinaloense*, *Ranchera*, *Sirreño*, *Sonidero*, and *Norteño*. He says that it's part of his culture and he enjoys it.

"C'mon, Ximena. You know that it's part of my culture. Of our culture," my dad says. "Yeah, Dad. You tell me all the time."

I am happy to be with my dad. I take his hand and we walk up the steps to the church. In the hall I see all the girls in the court of honor. They look me up and down.

I am irritated, but I enter the church with my dad, my mom, and my brothers. I don't like the idea of having to celebrate my cousin Paloma's *quinceañera*.

Chapter 8
Daniel

"Good morning, men. Are you ready to work with your new friends? They're waiting for you in the other room."

We hear the dogs barking from the other room. No one says anything, but we're all nervous. Normally we're only responsible for ourselves. But now we're going to have to take care of a dog for a few months. Sure, many of the men are fathers, but they aren't with their kids and they aren't familiar with that responsibility.

"Daniel, come here. Take this piece of paper. It has the information of the dog that you're going to train," the guard says.

I look at the paper. Here is the information:

Name: Dave
Color: black
Breed: mixed
Age: 9 months
Origin: Tennessee
Characteristics: timid, nervous

Dave? The dog's name is Dave? It's a bit odd, but that's okay.

With the paper, I go into the other room and I give it to the volunteer from the animal shelter.

"Hello," he says to me. "You're going to be working with Mr. Dave. He is a good dog, but you will need to have a lot of patience because he is very timid. Come with me, I'll introduce him to you."

We walk to the crate where Dave is. He is in the corner. He doesn't bark much, but he shakes a little.

The volunteer says to me that I can talk to him. "Put your hand next to the crate. Dave needs to smell you first."

I sit on the ground and I put my hand close to his nose. In that instant I see Dave's eyes. They're beautiful. His eyes are blue, light blue.

"They're the eyes of a Husky, right?" I ask the volunteer. "They're gorgeous."

"Yes. Mr. Dave has very pretty eyes. And yes, they are the eyes of a Husky. Spend a little more time with Dave. We are going to start class in 10 minutes."

All the other dogs bark with so much energy. Dave only uses his nose to get to know me a little more. The noise of the dogs is really loud, but I don't hear it. I am concentrating on my new friend. He needs me and I am going to help him.

Chapter 9
Ximena

After a long day celebrating my "perfect" cousin, I am both angry and sad when we get home. I go directly to my room and I take out my diary to write.

> *Dear diary,*
> *Today was terrible. I did not have a good time at Paloma's party. There were so many issues, particularly a conversation I had in the bathroom during the party:*
>
> *"Who are you?"*
> *"Hi. I'm Paloma's cousin."*
> *"Your dress is really ugly."*
> *"Yeah. And it's not new. It's obvious."*
> *"And your hair..."*
>
> *It was horrible. For five minutes the girls — all part of the court of honor — insulted me. Finally, I escaped. I went someplace else and cried.*

I'm still crying about the experience when my mom knocks on the door.

"Ximena, can I come in?" my mom asks.

"I don't want to talk to anyone," I respond.

"But, honey, I have something for you."

"What is it?" I ask my mom.

"A letter. Can I come in?"

"Okay," I say.

My mom comes in and gives me the letter.

"Ximena, it's a letter from your father, Daniel."

I take the envelope. I have no idea what to think. A letter from my biological father.

"Thanks, Mom. I'll read it now."

"Okay. If you want to talk to me..." my mom says.

"Okay. Thanks, Mom."

I open the envelope, take out the letter and start to read.

Dear Ximena,

I want to introduce myself. My name is Daniel. I am an inmate here at the Dudley Correctional Center. I am here for fifteen years because of an accident that happened thirteen years ago where a person died. You need to know the truth. I am sorry that I haven't contacted you until now. I didn't know about you. Though my aunt told me about you a while ago, at that time, I didn't like the person I was. I needed to change.

Now I am different than how I used to be. I want to tell you that I study a lot here. I take HVAC classes and now I am working in a program with dogs. Other guys and I train the dogs so that they can be adopted.

If you want to write back, I'd love to receive a letter from you. I'd love to get to know you. What is your favorite color? Do you like school? What activities do you like?

But you can decide if you'd like to write back or not. Also, you can ask any questions you'd like.

Sincerely,

Daniel

Wow. A letter from my biological father. This man is my father, but he's not my dad. And he's in prison. Only bad people are in prison. But I like his honesty. He's isn't offering me any excuses. I don't know how I feel about all this, but I am curious.

I get a piece of paper and begin to write.

Dear Daniel,

Thanks for writing to me. I'm Ximena. I am 13 years old. I have two brothers, Javier and Joaquín. I go to Crestview Middle School. I like to learn, but I don't like school much...

After writing for an hour, the story of my life is on paper. I put it in an envelope to send to Daniel.

Chapter 10
Daniel

Tonight, Dave and I are relaxing in the cell. I don't live with Johnny anymore. I needed more space since getting the dog. Besides, Johnny doesn't have the patience for a dog like Dave.

Dave is still very nervous, but he's good with me. He listens and pays attention when I talk. He is a good dog. He is nice and funny. And he is a good study partner.

"Dave," I say to him. "We need to study. I will review everything from my refrigeration course with you."

Dave looks at me, but he doesn't say anything. I start to read when Bear arrives at the door.

"Daniel, you have a letter from a new person," he calls at me.
"Thanks, Bear," I say.

I don't like that Bear makes comments about the mail, but it doesn't matter. I say to Dave,
"Dave! It's a letter from Ximena. Ximena is my daughter. I haven't met her... yet."

I am so happy. I read the whole letter to Dave. He looks at me with all his attention. It's a long letter with so many questions:

—*What happened the night of the accident?*
—*Were you alone?*
—*Why are you in prison for so long?*
—*What is prison like?*

And my favorite:

—*Can I visit you one day?*

Ximena tells me a lot about her life. She talks about problems that she has with her cousin's friends and many details about the *quinceañer*a. She mentions *quinceañeras* a lot in the letter but I don't know anything about these parties. They aren't part of my culture. Why are they so important?, I wonder. I'll ask her.

"Dave," I say, petting his head. "We're going to study later, but first we're going to write a letter to Ximena."

The dog doesn't say anything, he only raises his ears when I talk to him.

Dear Ximena,

Thank you for your very long letter. Now I know more about you, and in this letter I am going to answer your questions...

Chapter 11
Ximena

After Paloma's party, I have even more problems. Paloma's friends talk with the girls at my school and now everyone is talking about the situation at the *quinceañera* more than a month ago. Also, all the students know about my father, Daniel, and where he is.

"Your father is in prison."
"He's a criminal."
"You're just like him Ximena: bad, bad, bad."

The comments from the students are awful, and because of them, I'm not doing my homework and I'm not paying attention in class. So many people don't talk to me in school. I am really sad.

One day I get home from school and see my neighbor, Kendra. She is in her first year at San Dieguito Academy, a year older than me. She studies a lot, but she doesn't have many friends. She isn't popular. We aren't friends, but we talk when we see each other.

"Hi, Ximena," she says to me.
"Hey."
"How are you?" she asks.

I don't want to tell her the truth, but she already knows. Everyone knows my father is in prison.

"Good," I say. "How're you?"
"Well, we're preparing for my *quinceañera* in a few months. You're going to come, right?" she asks me.
"Of course, Kendra. I'd love to."
"And, Ximena, I want to invite you to be a member of my court of honor, if you'd like to," Kendra says.

I want to yell, "No, No, NO!", but I can't. It's difficult not having many friends (I know), and Kendra is a good person. She wants to have a great party too.

"Sure, Kendra. I'd love to. Thanks for inviting me to be part of your special day.

Let's talk later, okay? I need to go do my homework."

"Sounds good, Ximena. See you later," Kendra says.

Before going into my house, I look in the mailbox. There is a letter from Daniel. Good. I need to read some different news.

Daniel writes to me about his studies and the programs. He also tells me about his friends at the facility. He explains that they are good men who made bad decisions, but they are trying to change. It's a new perspective for me. Yes, people do bad things, but can they change? I don't know...

After reading the letter, I am more relaxed. I start a letter to Daniel.

Dear Daniel,

I am very happy to get your letter. Thank you for writing to me each week. I always am happy when there is a letter from you in the mailbox.

> *I'll tell you that I am not doing very well. I still am having problems with those girls from the party and other problems with other people from my school. I am really sad. And this afternoon, my neighbor Kendra invited me to participate in HER quinceañera. I didn't want to and I don't want to, but she doesn't have anyone else to invite. She isn't very popular at school. So, I told her yes. I'm going to have to tell my mom.*
>
> *And you? How're you doing? The dog? Do you have a picture with Dave? And, can I visit you one day?*

I finish the letter and put it in an envelope with the address to Dudley and the number of prisoner Daniel, 7042-99DRQ. Tomorrow I will put it in the mailbox for the mailman.

Chapter 12
Daniel

Something is happening in Dudley today because we are in a state of emergency, or a lockdown. No one can leave their cells and there aren't any classes or programs today. I have permission to leave with Dave once in the morning and once in the afternoon to go for a pee (Dave, not me), but we won't have classes with the trainer today.

"Dave," I say, "it's a good day to write a letter to Ximena, don't you think?"

Dave looks at me with his light blue eyes and lifts his ears, but he doesn't say anything. I take out a piece of paper and start writing.

Dear Ximena,

I have a lot of time to write to you today because the prison is in lockdown. The guards are conducting investigations and no one can leave their cells. I am here with Dave (of course). He says hello. He is a completely different dog now. He is learning from me, but I am learning a lot from him, too. Now Dave knows my voice and understands my commands:

Sit
Stay
Come
Lie Down

And he also gives me his paw when I say, "high five." Ha, ha! He is very intelligent and a lot less nervous than he used to be.

I'm teaching Dave a lot, but he's teaching me too. He's teaching me patience and unconditional love. I like him a lot. There are only three more weeks in the program. :(Dave is a good friend. I'll miss him a lot.

I'm sorry for the problems that you're having in school. I don't like to give advice (and I'm not really in a position to give it to you), but continue with patience.

> *This will pass and everything will be okay. I know because before I had a lot of problems and now I don't have as many.*

While I write the letter to Ximena, I have a phenomenal idea. I need to contact her mom and her stepfather first. It's such an excellent idea!

I finish the letter to Ximena and I put a photo in the envelope as well. I am going to have to wait until tomorrow to send it, but that's no problem. It gives me more time to write to Marisol and Federico.

Chapter 13
Ximena

My mom comes to my school today for a meeting with my math and science teachers. I have bad grades in those classes. I am also at the meeting. I don't want to be at this meeting, but my mom insisted. It's difficult to be in a meeting with three adults.

"Ms. Meléndez, Ximena is a good girl and she is very smart. But she isn't doing the homework in my class," my math teacher says.
"She's also not doing the work in science class. She has bad grades. How can we help you, Ximena?" my science teacher asks.

I don't want to respond to Mr. Kelley, but he is very nice.

"The work isn't hard, Mr. Kelley. I just don't have the motivation to do it," I say.

I know I didn't answer his question, but I don't have any idea how he can help me.

The meeting ends when I promise them that I will try to work harder in their classes.

In the car my mom tries to talk to me, but I don't pay attention. I don't know what's the matter with me. I don't want to do homework, I don't want to leave my room, I don't want to do anything.

*****

We arrive home and I go directly to the mailbox. Today there are two letters from Daniel, one for me and another for my parents. Normally Daniel doesn't write to my parents. Hmmm...

I take the letter for me and I go to my room to read it. In the envelope there is a photo of a dog. I read the letter for the explanation.

Daniel writes me about a lockdown that occurred in Dudley. He couldn't leave his cell for two days, only so Dave could go out.. *Dave needs to pee*, Daniel explains to me.

He also writes about his graduation and about the program with the dogs.

I'm sending you a photo of Dave. I wanted to send you another photo of my graduation, but I don't have one. But now, with the HVAC certificate, I can get a better job here in Dudley.

Daniel has a hard life. My life is easy in comparison, so, why am I so sad?

As always, Daniel asks me a few questions at the end of the letter. Though I don't have any motivation to do much, I always write him back.

Dear Daniel,
The picture of Dave is fantastic! He looks like a very good dog, despite his nervousness. Why is he so nervous?
You asked me why quinceañeras *are so important. I'll explain.*
The quinceañera *is a ritual for many Hispanic girls. It's the celebration where a girl becomes a woman. Before, it was a celebration to show that girls were ready to get married, but now it symbolizes the transition from girlhood to a womanhood.*

For me it's a connection to my culture and my religion. If I'm honest, I don't want to be a little girl anymore. I want to be an adult. I still have a lot of problems in school, in my classes, and with other students.

Since my birthday two months ago I've started thinking about my quinceañera. For my party next year, I want a celebration different from Paloma's. I don't want a show. I want a simple ceremony and a simple party. I know that my mom and my dad don't have much money, but I would love an elegant dress. Light blue. With lots of flowers. I want to be a princess for a day.

Next month I will go to my neighbor Kendra's quinceañera. I am one of the girls in her court. I'm going to that party to get more ideas for mine.

I finish the letter when my mom knocks on the door. "Ximena, can I come in?"

I don't want to talk to my mom, but I respond, "Yes."

My mom and I talk for an hour — about school, about my father Daniel, and about my problems in school, with my classes and with my classmates. She wants to help me, and I need help.

"Ximena, what do you think about adopting a dog?" my mom asks.

I look at her with surprise.

"What?" I ask. Javier, Joaquín, and I really want a dog, but my parents always tell us 'no.'
"Yes, honey. You and your brothers are older and need the responsibility. And to have a 'friend' like a dog will be very helpful for you, I think," my mom says.
"Oh, Mom! That's an excellent idea. Thank you!"
I give her a big hug.

"But don't say anything to your brothers yet. I need to talk to your dad first."

My mom is going to convince my dad really fast, because my dad wants a dog too. He loves dogs. I do too.

What kind of dog will we adopt?

Chapter 14
Daniel

I return from my new job as a technician here in prison. Along with a supervisor, a group of men and I work in a workshop in here where we repair the machines. I like the work.

Bear is at the door of my cell with a few letters for me.

"Hello, Daniel. How is your new job? I have some letters for you. Ximena wrote you another one."
"Hi, Bear. Work is really good, thanks," I say.
"And Dave, how are you?" Bear asks Dave.
I respond, "Dave is good. He is alone a lot of the day right now. I don't like it, but it's part of the training. And he will be adopted soon."
"Oh, really?"
"Yeah, Ximena's mom and her family are going to adopt him."

Normally I don't talk much with the other guys in the prison about personal things, but I am so happy. Dave is going to be part of Ximena's life.

"Wow. That's great, Daniel. When?" Bear asks me.

"In two weeks. Ximena doesn't know. It's a surprise."

"I like that news, Daniel. Good luck," Bear says.

Bear gives me the letters and a smile. Sometimes he's a little nosy, but he is a good person. A lot of the men here are good people, people who have had problems. Like me.

Dave is by my side when I sit on my bed to read the letters. One letter is from Ximena and the other is from the parole board. I only have one more year of my sentence, and I need to prepare a lot of documents and papers for my hopeful parole.

"Dave," I say to the dog, "you are going to leave here before me, but I am going to leave too."

Dave looks at me with his light blue eyes, but he doesn't say anything. He is a good dog and a good friend.

I pet his head and open the envelope to read my daughter's letter.

Dear Daniel,

I have good news. My mom said that we can adopt a dog! I want a black dog like Dave. He is very handsome. :) :) :)

The letter has a lot of information about the life of a teenager. Ximena says that she's still having problems at school, but I can tell that she is so excited to adopt a dog that I notice a different tone in her letter.

I am happy and I say to the dog, "Dave. you are going to live with Ximena and her brothers. What do you think?"

Dave looks at me and lifts his ears, and this time it looks like he has a smile.

Chapter 15
Ximena

"Hey, Ximena."

"Hi, Mom."

"How was your day?" my mom asks me.

She picks me up from the lessons that I have for Kendra's *quinceañera*. We have to practice two times a week for two months. Today we practiced *el vals*[1].

"So-so. I'm hungry. What's for dinner?"

"We are going to pick up pizza, but first we need to go to the city," my mom says.

"That far and with so much traffic? Mom, I don't want to," I say to my mom.

"Ximena, I'm sorry but we have an appointment."

"You didn't tell me before. Why?" I say, mad.

My mom doesn't look at me but she has a big smile. What's going on? Where are we going?

---

[1] vals: waltz.

"Mom, where are we going?" I ask.

"You'll see."

The traffic is horrible at this hour, but I don't say anything. I look at pictures of *quinceañeras* on Instagram on my phone.

We arrive and I am the one with a smile now. We're at an animal shelter.

"Mom, are we going to adopt a dog today?" I ask.

"Yes, Ximena. Let's go."

My mom goes to the reception desk and talks with the woman. She pays some money and fills out two forms. After fifteen minutes, a man comes to out with a dog. He isn't very big, but he isn't small. He has ocean blue eyes. He is black with some white... It's...it's Dave!

"Dave!" I yell. I sit on the ground to pet him. Dave is a little nervous, but after a few minutes he relaxes a bit.

"Mom, thank you," I say. I start to cry. "Thank you, Mom. Thank you."

I hug my new friend. I am so happy.

*****

After an exciting night with Dave in the house, the two of us are in my room. Dave is on the floor close to me when I write a letter to Daniel. I write about Dave (of course!), the lessons for Kendra's *quinceañera* and my *quinceañera* in eight months.

At the end I ask a question:

> *Daniel, I'd like to visit you. Is that possible? I am going to ask my mom about it soon!*

Chapter 16
Daniel

Ximena's letter has many hearts and smiley faces. She is very happy with Dave. The two are spending a lot of time together. They go for walks in the park and participate in a program to visit a local nursing home. Dave is perfect for the program because he's nice and he doesn't have too much energy. And he has such beautiful eyes! No one can resist his eyes.

I am a bit sad that Dave isn't with me. I concentrate on my work so I don't think of the dog.

*****

In the workshop this morning at work, there is a problem. A big problem.

"Daniel, I need to talk with you," another man at work tells me. Another prisoner.
"What's up?" I ask.
"A machine is going to arrive tomorrow and I need to repair it," he tells me.

The man describes the machine to me.

I don't say anything, but the situation isn't good. This man has a bad reputation. Infamous. He says that he's getting drugs from the workshop and is selling them in prison. But I don't want to get myself involved in problems. I have seven months before I go before the patrol board and I don't want any infractions on my record.

But the informal rules of prisoners are sometimes more important than the formal rules.

What do I do?

Chapter 17
Ximena

Finally, the day of Kendra's *quinceañera* has arrived. I am wearing a used dress from Flashbacks that is a color that Kendra likes.

We practiced dancing for two months. Now I know all the steps for each part well for when I dance with the other boys and girls in the court, especially *el vals* and the surprise dance. But first we all need to accompany Kendra to the special mass in church.

"Ximena, are you ready?" my dad asks me.

The whole family is going to the mass and Kendra's party. Kendra's mom and my mom are friends. My mom likes to help, so she prepared a lot of food for the day:

enchiladas[2], picadillo[3], and tamales[4]. The tamales that my mom makes are the best.

"Yes, Dad. I'm ready," I say from my room. "Let's go!"
I pat Dave's head and leave my room.

"Princess. How beautiful you are." my dad says when he sees me.

The smile that I have now is real. A lot has changed in the last few months. Everything is a lot better at school: my classes are good and I have more confidence. Dave has helped me a lot.

*****

I like to go to church, especially to celebrate a friend. I am very happy and I feel happy — for me and for Kendra. Kendra is happy as well. Now she has more friends.

---

[2] enchiladas: corn filled tortillas covered with chili pepper sauce.
[3] picadillo: Latin American dish similar to hash.
[4] tamales: Meso-American dough-filled food, steamed in corn husks or banana leaves.

After spending a lot of time together in at the dance lessons, we are all good friends. At the beginning it was hard to convince the boys to participate, but at the end they enjoyed themselves.

At the mass, Kendra's godparents give her a rosary and her parents give her a necklace of the virgin of Guadalupe, the patron saint of Mexico. Kendra also gets a tiara to indicate that she will always be a princess. Kendra is so beautiful! And so happy.

After the mass I talk with Kendra before going to the party.

"Kendra, you look so beautiful today. I'm really happy for you."
"Ximena," she says to me. "Thank you for being my friend. I am happy too. We're going to have fun at the party. Are you ready?"
"Yes! We're going to dance a lot," I say, with a real smile.

La entrada[5] to the party is excellent. The girls and boys of the court enter the room first and then Kendra comes in. Her party has some traditional parts, but Kendra has included her own ideas too. She wanted the formal part of the church, but the party itself is less traditional. We enter to the song "Quinceañera" by Thalia. The rhythm is a little slow, but it's okay. We have a surprise for later.

At the end of la entrada, Kendra's godfather makes a toast.

"Thank you all for coming to celebrate Kendra's *quinceañera*. Here we are to accept her, for the first time, as a woman. Kendra, you are so special; to us and to everyone here. I hope that life loves you as we all love you."

Other people talk as well.

---

[5] la entrada: the entrance; how the celebrant and her court enter the room where the party is held.

Afterwards Kendra dances with her dad to "Tiempo de vals" by Chayanne. He cries, but he is very happy and very proud. Kendra cries a bit. She is happy, too, but she doesn't want to ruin her makeup.

Finally, it's time to dance the surprise dance that we had practiced for months. We dance to the song, "Mi Gente" by J Balvin and Willy William. It's very different from *los vals*. The guys have sunglasses on and look very handsome. They didn't want to participate in the court at the beginning, but now they are going to dance!

The dance is very exciting. We dance to a mix of songs for ten minutes. We have a lot of fun. And we dance REALLY well. At the end Kendra takes the microphone and says:

"Thank you all for coming. But I want to say a special thank you to my friends here," she looks at us and says, "I have enjoyed getting to know you better and dancing with you all. Now, let's eat!"

The music continues and the people dance. Other people go to the tables with the food. There is so much food that the mothers prepared to help Kendra's family. It's a tradition to help the other families preparing the food, and because the moms know how to cook, the food is amazing!

There aren't any more ceremonies during the party. Before, Kendra and I chatted a lot about the preparations and the plans. She didn't want to do the shoe changing ceremony from flats to heels, nor did she want to do the last doll ceremony based on the Mayan tradition where a girl leaves her last doll to show that she has become a woman. Instead, she has a few traditional elements and other modern ones.

It was a phenomenal day. I enjoyed it a lot.

*****

At home I talk with my parents about my *quinceañera*.

"Mom. Dad. I don't want a party like Paloma's because I know that it's not possible for the family. I would like a party more like the one today. Can I?"

My dad speaks first. "Ximena, you are going to have the party that you want, if it's possible. I will work more to be able to give you that party."

He takes my hand and gives me a kiss on the head.

"Thanks, Dad," I say.

But I see my mom's face. It's obvious that there is another problem.

Chapter 18
Daniel

I am preparing to go to work in the prison. I wash my face and brush my teeth. I think of the problem at work. I still don't know what to do.

If I tell the guards, I am going to have a lot of problems with the other prisoners. If I don't say anything, I could have more problems with getting my freedom. And I only have five more months here. A few more months and I can be with my daughter: walk in the park, eat ice cream, attend her *quinceañera*...

*****

When I arrive at work, the bad guy watches me a lot. He doesn't trust me. When I go to talk to the boss, the man stops me and threatens me. In his hand he has a shiv, or a prison-made knife. He talks to me with such ugly words and an ugly voice.

"Daniel, don't you dare say anything to anyone about these machines. You will not say anything. If you do, I will kill you."

The man has the blade to my stomach. I don't say anything.

Finally, he turns around and returns to work. I do too. I don't talk to the boss because I am scared and nervous.

The rest of the day that man watches me with his black eyes.

In my fourteen years here at Dudley I have had problems, but they were problems that I caused myself because of my attitude and being immature. However, this time I'm not looking for problems. I don't want them. I want to leave Dudley. I want to start a new life.

Still, I don't want problems with the guards. What do I do?

*****

After a long day, I return to my cell. There is a letter from Ximena. I smile, even though I'm really nervous.

Dear Daniel,

Thank you for your letter. Dave and I are good. He is here and says hello. Ha, ha!

School is good too. My grades are good and I have more friends. And Dave and I spend a few hours at the nursing home on the weekends. There is a woman there that likes Dave a lot. She is from the Philippines and she talks to Dave in Filipino. It's beautiful to listen to.

I read more of the letter. My daughter is happy, but everything is not okay. It's not awful, but there's a problem.

Daniel, I am looking for a dress for my quinceañera. There is a VERY beautiful one on Celia's Creation's in Chula Vista. Kendra and I ate ice cream one day at

Handles and we saw it looking at pictures on Instagram. It's beautiful: it's light blue with so many beautiful decorations. I mentioned it to my mom and her first question was: How much does it cost? I know that my family doesn't have a lot of money. I am sad. I really want the dress, but it's not possible for me to get it.

It's obvious that Ximena wants the dress.

And I want to help.

Can I help?

Yes, I can. I have an idea.

Chapter 19
Ximena

We begin the preparations for my party. My mom calls all of her friends and they come to prepare the food; *picadillo* and *pernil*[6]. My dad's cousin who is a DJ, is going to do the music. That day we will first go to the church for the mass and then to my godparents' house for the party. The party will be on their patio.

One afternoon my mom and I are at the In-N-Out close to our house. We eat hamburgers, French fries, and shakes. My mom is very happy about the party. I am happy too, but I can't stop thinking about the dress.

"Mom, are we going to have tables and chairs for the patio?" I ask my mom.
"Of course, Ximena. The people need to sit to eat," my mom says, laughing.
"But my godparents don't have that many on their patio. What are we going to do?"

---

[6] pernil: slow-roasted marinated pork shoulder or pork leg.

"Don't worry. We are going to rent tables and chairs," she explains.

"How much money does it cost?" I ask.

"Ay, Ximena. Don't worry about the money. You will have a beautiful party," my mom says to me.

I have a lot of questions, but I don't say a word. If there is enough money for tables and chairs, why isn't there enough for the dress?

*****

We get home and there is a letter from Daniel. The letter says that he is working a lot and he likes his work. But he doesn't write much. He must be working a lot.

I want to write in my diary about my feelings about the money, the dress, and my party, but I decide to write a letter to Daniel. I talk about the preparations for the party, the food, and the music. I don't mention the dress. At the end I ask just one question:

When can I come to Dudley to visit you?

With love,
Ximena

Chapter 20
Daniel

Today is the day. I am going to talk to my boss about the drugs. I hope that they believe me. It's a huge risk.

"Mr. Meyer. Can I talk with you?" I ask my boss. Mr. Meyer is the civilian boss and isn't a prison guard.
"Of course, Daniel. What's going on?" Mr. Meyer says to me. "Is everything okay?"
"Uh, not exactly. Can we talk in the office?" I ask him.
"Yes, let's go."

Mr. Meyer gives instructions to the other men while the two of us to into his office. I can't waste the chance, so I start to talk.

"Mr. Meyer, there are some men that are using their jobs to get drugs in prison. Someone outside puts them into the machines that we repair and..."

My boss doesn't let me continue.

"Daniel. We already know. Thank you for saying something. The guards are conducting an investigation, but need more time to resolve the problem. You only have a few more months here in Dudley, right?"

"Yes, sir. Five months. I want to get out so that I can go to my daughter's *quinceañera*," I say with a little smile.

"Well, do your work and don't say anything to anyone. You are a good man, Daniel. Honest. You've changed a lot," he says to me.

"Thank you, sir."

"Now get back to work and keep your mouth shut," he says.

"Sounds good. Thank you. And one more thing?"

"What is it?" the boss asks me with curiosity.

"I'd like to give the money that I earn from this job to my daughter. Is that possible?"

"Let me ask about that, Daniel."

"Great, boss. Thank you. She wants a very special dress for her party," I say with a bigger smile.

I return to work. Like the boss said to me, I do my work and I don't say anything. I think about the money that I want to send to my daughter for the dress. I earn about a dollar an hour, but I want to help her. I think of my parole as well. Will they give it to me? I want to attend Ximena's party, but I don't know if I will be released, or even if I will be invited.

The letter that I get from Ximena is a lot shorter than normal.

> *Dear Daniel,*
>
> *My parents told me that they are going to bring me to the prison to see you in two weeks. I can't wait.*
>
> *Hugs,*
>
> *Ximena and Dave*

Two weeks. Two weeks to get the money together. Two weeks before I'll see my daughter, and meet her for the first time.

Chapter 21
Ximena

One day Dave and I prepare ourselves to go to the nursing home when my mom comes into my room and sits on my bed.

"Xime, I need to talk to you," she says, worried.

"What's wrong, Mom? You sound very serious."

"There was an accident in the prison. We can't go visit Daniel tomorrow," she explains to me, without really explaining anything.

"But Daniel is okay, right?" I ask. I am now very worried too.

"No, Ximena. Daniel is not okay. He is in the prison hospital. He was attacked. Stabbed. He is not okay. He isn't conscious right now."

"But Mom. He can't die. I haven't gotten to meet him," I say, yelling.

"I know, baby. There isn't anything more we can do, only wait and pray."

I cry, but I don't know why. It's true that I didn't know Daniel, but he IS my father. From the letters that I wrote and received, I learned more about myself. I want to know him. He has to get better. I hope so.

*****

I am sad when I arrive at the nursing home, but Dave is VERY happy. He wags his tail and his butt to show it.

First, we go to visit Mrs. Santos, the Filipino woman. She is in her room drinking tea. She is surprised to see us.
"Hi, Mrs. Santos. How are you?"

Mrs. Santos is 92 years old. She says that mentally she is doing great, but physically...

"And how're you, Ximena?" she asks me. "Are you sad today?"
"Yes, ma'am. My father, the one that's in prison, isn't doing well."
"Come tell me everything, Ximena. What happened?" Mrs. Santos says.

Dave and I sit close to the old woman and I tell her everything.

Mrs. Santos is very smart. Sometimes she tells me some Filipino sayings that help me with my problems. Today she tells me another.

"Remember, Ximena, *Habang may buhay, may pag-asa*. When there is life, there is hope."
"That's true, Mrs. Santos. You have told me a lot of the story of your life and I have learned a lot. Thank you. I am going to think about that saying — but not in Filipino. It's very hard. Ha, ha!"
"Yes, Filipino is different than Spanish, but *Ang hindi marunong magmahal sa sariling wika, ay mahigit pa sa mabaho at malansang isda*. The person that doesn't love their native language is as poor as a rotten fish."
"Ay, Mrs. Santos. That one is longer than the other saying," I say, smiling.
"Thank you for visiting me, Ximena and Dave. I hope that your father gets better.

Now, go home and write a letter to your father," Mrs. Santos says.

And as usual, I listen to the old woman.

Chapter 22
Daniel

I am still in clinic at Dudley. I was unconscious for two days. It was a horrible situation, but now I am better. I want to leave the clinic so that I can return to work. I want to earn more money for Ximena.

Everything is arranged. I will be able to give the money that is in my account to Ximena. She wants that pretty dress for her *quinceañera*, and I want her to have it.

"Hi, Daniel. Good morning. How are you feeling today?" Dr. Allen asks me.

"Good morning. I'm a lot better, thanks Doctor," I say.

"I can see that. I'll let you return to general population today," she says to me.

"That's good, Doctor. And when can I return to work?"

"Next week. You will be a lot stronger in a few days."

"Thanks, Doctor. Thank you for everything."

*****

In the afternoon I am in my cell. I still don't have a cellie[7], I'm here alone. I miss Dave.

Bear comes to the door with the mail.

"Hey, Daniel. It's good to see you again. How are you?" he says, yelling.
"Hi, Bear. Yeah, it was a few hard days. But I'm doing better now," I say.
"They told me that they hit you really hard at work."
"Yeah, I was unconscious for two days."
"Don't worry about those dudes. They transferred them to another prison. And fast," Bear tells me.
"That's good news," I say. "Do you have something for me?"
"Oh, yes! Two letters. One from Ximena and the other from Marisol."
"Thanks, man."

I sit on my bed. My head still hurts a little. Well, really my entire body aches. Those

---

[7] cellie: colloquial term for prison roommate.

dudes from the workshop hit me really hard.

I open Marisol's letter first.

Dear Daniel,

I hope that you are well. They tell me that you were unconscious in the clinic. Ximena is very worried about you — and I am too. Ximena has changed a lot in the last few months. The relationship she has with you is very important for her and her identity. Thank you for being so good with her, your daughter. And I'm sorry for not telling her about you before.

We will be traveling to Dudley next Saturday. Federico, Ximena and I will all go. It's important that we all get to know each other.

Marisol

Wow! In a week I am going to meet my daughter for the first time.

Chapter 23
Ximena

It's Saturday, the day that we're going to Dudley to meet my father. It takes an hour to get to there. I don't talk much in the car and my dad notices.

"Ximena, are you nervous?" my dad asks me.
"Yes. A little. What happens if he doesn't like me?"
"Ximena, your father already loves you. Like I love you," my dad says.
"Yeah, I know. It's just a little weird that I'm meeting my father after 15 years."
"It's going to be a good experience for you," my mom says, smiling. "For all of us."

On the walk to the prison I think about the problems that I've had and how I've resolved them. Many times I wrote in my diary or wrote a letter to Daniel and I felt better. Writing has helped me a lot.

Finally, we arrive, but we need to wait longer. It's a very long process to visit a prisoner. You need to talk to officials, show identification, and wait. And wait more. It's awful.

After two hours, an official calls us, "Visitors for Daniel..."

At that moment I see Daniel. I see my father. He is in the visiting room. He still has some bruises on his face and neck, but he also has a big smile.

"Hello, Ximena. I am Daniel," he says to me.
"I know," I say, also smiling. You sent me photos, remember? Ha, ha!"
"Of course. I'm sorry. I'm a bit nervous," Daniel says to me.
"Me too," I admit. "My parents are here too. You already know my mom and that is Federico. My dad."
"Nice to meet you, Daniel," my dad says. "Ximena is a very special girl."

Daniel doesn't say anything. He looks at my mom. Finally, he says, "Marisol. Ximena is beautiful. She looks exactly like you."

"Thank you, Daniel. We are very proud of her."

Daniel talks now. "Marisol. Federico. Thank you for being so great. Ximena is very lucky to have you."

"We are going to celebrate her in a few months at her party," my dad says.

"Yeah, Daniel. My *quinceañera* is in January. Will you be able to go?"

"I know that I mentioned it was a possibility, but I don't think it is now. The process of leaving prison is very long. I won't be able to go."

I am a bit sad to hear the news. I would've liked to celebrate with Daniel too.

"But," Daniel says, "I have other news. Ximena, do you already have your dress for the party?"

I don't know why he asks me. Daniel knows about the problem with the dress. The dress that I want is very expensive.

"No. I need to find one..." I say.

"Don't worry. Although I don't know much about *quinceañeras*, I know that the dress is very important to you. Tomorrow go to the store to buy it. I sent the money you needed to your mom."

"What? How?" I say, surprised. My mom doesn't say anything. "Mom?"

"It's true, Xime. Your father," she says, looking at Daniel, "has sent me money. We're going shopping tomorrow."

"But how? From your job?" I ask Daniel.

"Yes, Ximena. I don't earn much, but all the money that I've earned..."

"Ay, thank you, Daniel!" I grab his hand. I want to give him a hug, but it's not allowed. "Thank you!"

We talk for an hour longer. Much of the time we talk about the party. I'm really happy. I'm happy about the dress and the party, but I am also so happy that I finally met my father. He is a good person. He needs to learn more about Hispanic culture, but he is a good person. Ha, ha!

Finally, we say goodbye.

"Daniel, thank you for the dress. I will send you photos."

"You will be a princess, I know," Daniel says, looking at my dad.

"She is our princess," Federico says, offering his hand to Daniel. "Yours too."

"Daniel, thank you," my mom says, her eyes filled with tears.

My mom and Daniel take each other's hands too. And now she takes mine. I take Daniel's hand.

"Daniel, I am so happy that you are in my life now. Thank you for helping me so much."
"I feel the same, Ximena. Thank you for changing my life."

I cry a little, but I am very happy,

"I will send you photos, Daniel. And more of Dave."
"Sounds good, Ximena," he says to me. "And say hi to Dave. See you next time."

As I leave the visitors room I say goodbye with a wave one more time and I say, "Bye, Dad," but there is too much noise so he doesn't hear me.

ABOUT THE AUTHOR

Jennifer Degenhardt taught high school Spanish for over 20 years and now teaches at the college level. At the time she realized her own high school students, many of whom had learning challenges, acquired language best through stories, so she began to write ones that she thought would appeal to them. She has been writing ever since.

Other titles by Jen Degenhardt available on Amazon:

La chica nueva | La Nouvelle Fille | <u>The New Girl</u>
La chica nueva (the ancillary/workbook
volume, Kindle book, audiobook)
Chuchotenango
El jersey | <u>The Jersey</u> | *Le Maillot*
La mochila | <u>The Backpack</u>
Moviendo montañas
La vida es complicada
Quince | <u>Fifteen</u>
El viaje difícil | *Un Voyage Difficile* | <u>A Difficult Journey</u>
La niñera
Fue un viaje difícil
Con (un poco de) ayuda de mis amigos
La última prueba
Los tres amigos | <u>Three Friends</u> | *Drei Freunde* | *Les Trois Amis*
María María: un cuento de un huracán | <u>María María: A Story of a Storm</u> | Maria Maria: un histoire d'un orage
Debido a la tormenta
La lucha de la vida | <u>The Fight of His Life</u>
Secretos
Como vuela la pelota

@JenniferDegenh1

@jendegenhardt9

@puenteslanguage &
World LanguageTeaching Stories (group)

Visit www.puenteslanguage.com to sign up to receive
information on new releases and other events.

Check out all titles as ebooks with audio on
www.digilangua.co.

Made in the USA
Columbia, SC
07 February 2022